I am Beautiful

Kristin Drosdick

BookLeaf
Publishing

India | USA | UK

Presentation by *BookLeaf Publishing*

Web: www.bookleafpub.com

E-mail: info@bookleafpub.com

ISBN: 978-93-5744-954-0

First edition 2022

DEDICATION

I dedicate this book to my dad, Jim, and my grandfather, Bud. Thank you both for always being there for me and loving me unconditionally. I love you.

ACKNOWLEDGEMENT

Thank you to everyone I have encountered while on this journey. Each of you have taught me a lesson about life and more about myself. If it wasn't for all of you, then I wouldn't be the person I am today and for that I am eternally grateful.

I am Beautiful

I look in the mirror
Content as can be
I am beautiful
As I see

My world around me
Can be mean and cruel
Insecurities and doubts
Used as fuel

Look in my eyes
My soul, I see
Feel the light
Abundance is free

I am Listening

I close my eyes
What do I feel?
I am wise
Trust this is real

Soak in the pain
Breathe and relax
It's time to gain
All of the facts

What's my lesson?
Soul, I hear you reply
Continue progression
An answer to my why

The visions I see
The words I hear
Attentive, be free
Trust without fear

Release the past
Give thanks and let go
Patience comes fast
Go with the flow

To Thine Own Self Be True

I know my truth
I feel the knowing deep inside
Release and be free
Flowing along for the ride

As I See

I am beautiful
As I see
Vibrant as a tree

I am beautiful
As I feel
Authentic and real

I am beautiful
As I know
Full of glow

I am beautiful
As I see
Content and free

The Process

Rising up, I feel this pain
Questioning, "What's to gain?"
My heart is full of dark and hurt
Self love and worth, I assert
My energy, exerting all around
Reminding myself to ground
What am I feeling? Why so low?
Envisioning my light, extending that glow
Betrayal of self, how did I get here?
I must dive in to process without fear
Trust the Universe, as it makes me full
Go within, process and you'll
Benefit from my radiant light
Freedom and abundance is our right

Direction

Our journey, this life, a lesson
Dive deep within and there is no guessing
I ask, "Soul, what do you have to say?"
Teach me, guide me, throughout each day
Fill my heart and soul with light
Release, be free; no struggle or fight

Purpose

Guide me soul, lead the way
Each moment that makes today
Stay conscious and present
Actions and decisions, I'll never regret it
Moving forward, keep steady
Abundance and freedom, I'm ready
To live the life that's meant for me
Alive, loving on others and free

Respect

Released the toxic
Evolution in divine timing
Spiritual growth
Proudly spoken words
Expressed boundaries
Chaos free
Transformed

Foundations

Respect
Full force in effect
Self love is true
Roots that grew
Into a tree
Divine and free
Mirrored that past
Released and fast
Thankful for light
Loved all with might
Soul driven
Carefully scriven
Glad to be me
Loving and free

Wake Up

It's time to realize
The hurt within one's eyes

Release and be free
To let it be

A hurt that is mine
Knowing all will be fine

Releasing dark from one's heart
Must be the start

Time for a new beginning
Light is winning

The battle within
Time to win

Joyfulness is key
Just let it be

Universe will tell
All is well

Choose life with each moment

Learning from it

A new life
Releasing negative rife

A chance to be taken
Trembled and shaken

Release and be free
Let it all be

Grammie's Love

You made your presence strong today
Before, you felt so far away
Your spirit touched my heart
Light made into art
A flood of memories flowed around
Tears of loss were found
A gentle reminder you're still near
And there's nothing to fear
I felt you say to let life be
And you're always here with me

I am the Light

Selfishness is gold
Hear the truth be told

I am the light
Let there be no fight

All is meant to be
Fill my heart with glee

Love is all around
Roots deep within the ground

Reminding you
All is true

Face my darkness
With a sweet kiss

Once released
Say goodbye to the beast

And live my life free
The way it's meant to be

Full of love and grace

Shown in my face

Be that example
Never ramble

About the dark
That filled my heart

Follow the good
As the light would

Remember my gold
Abundance will unfold

To You

That moment when you realize
The truth is meant to be
Realizing the heartache
Release and be free

Time will always tell
The truth that has been
Letting go of failure
Seek it within

Go deep and realize
It's out of your control
Time and energy
Always go with the flow

Look within
You did everything you could
Love, kindness, and ears
It's time to let go

The past from all these years
Stay abundant
And stay free
Love and light

With thee
Set yourself free
From the control
And let it be

Meant To Be

Diving deep
Into one's soul
What's left
Than to let go

Of all the hurt
One once felt
Tucked away
Tied up with a belt

Let it go
And feel free
Nothing left
Just let it be

Replace the old
With the new
Tried and told
As the wind blew

A new breath of life
Into the deep
Love
One must keep

Fill it up
Don't let go
Be myself
And watch it glow

Into the one
One's meant to be

Focus

Self love is true
Holding through
The good and bad
Always stay glad
Focusing on myself
Building true wealth
Releasing the dark
Filling my heart
Full of love and joy
Ruler of my ploy
Breathe and be free
Being selflessly me

The Secrets

I hold the key to my own fate
Protector of my gate
Guard my mind, heart and soul
Abundance is the goal
Easily attained
By releasing what has drained
The energy from my view
Release all I know to be true
These are the secrets to an abundant life
Free from strife

Lead the Way

Soul, I see your guiding path
Feel and release this life's wrath
I feel you know the way
To live each moment in today
I feel I'm meant to have more
Beautifully abundant, for sure

Never Alone

As I sit in silence
Thinking, "Why this?"
All the hurt and pain
From people, I refrain
Why do I feel so lonely,
With people all around me?
Different, I guess I'm meant to be
I've lost my roots, like a dying tree
Then, I feel my soul as an energetic tone
Reminding me I'm not alone
Feel the joy and smile
I was never alone all the while
I'm meant to feel the dark and release
For myself and others to feel peace

Transformation

As I stare up at the night stars
I'm reminded this life is ours
To be content, abundant and free
Declare it! Make it a decree
To live each moment as if it's the last
Staying present, letting go of the past
Simply know that with my transformation
I change and empower the nation
To rise up and be the light
This truth is everyone's right

The Light

24

Follow the light
It brightens the path
No need for might
Nor wrath

These lessons I'll learn
Along the way
Let the darkness burn
Do as I say

True Love

Throughout all the travel
I'm going to unravel
Your most inner being
It's truly worth seeing

This feeling inside
Used as a guide
Listening to my soul
True love is the goal

An abundant connection is built
For generations, it will be felt

www.ingramcontent.com/pod-product-compliance
Lightning Source LLC
LaVergne TN
LVHW021349200726